Thomas Thornely

The Ethical and Social Aspect of Habitual Confession to a Priest

Thomas Thornely

The Ethical and Social Aspect of Habitual Confession to a Priest

ISBN/EAN: 9783337331184

Printed in Europe, USA, Canada, Australia, Japan

Cover: Foto ©Lupo / pixelio.de

More available books at **www.hansebooks.com**

THE
ETHICAL AND SOCIAL ASPECT

OF

HABITUAL CONFESSION TO A PRIEST,

BY

THOMAS THORNELY, B.A., LL.M.

LIGHTFOOT AND WHEWELL SCHOLAR IN THE UNIVERSITY OF CAMBRIDGE,
LAW STUDENT OF TRINITY HALL, AND INNS OF COURT STUDENT
IN JURISPRUDENCE AND ROMAN CIVIL LAW.

London:
MACMILLAN AND CO.
1880

[The Right of Translation is reserved.]

Cambridge:
PRINTED BY C. J. CLAY, M.A.,
AT THE UNIVERSITY PRESS.

ADVERTISEMENT.

The late Richard Burney, Esq., M.A., of Christ's College, Cambridge, previously to his death on the 30th Nov. 1845, empowered his Cousin, Mr Archdeacon Burney, to offer, through the Vice-Chancellor, to the University of Cambridge, the sum of £3,500 Reduced Three per Cent. Stock, for the purpose of establishing an Annual Prize, to be awarded to the Graduate who should produce the best Essay on a subject to be set by the Vice-Chancellor.

On the day after this offer was communicated to the Vice-Chancellor, Mr Burney died; but his sister and execuutrix, Miss J. Caroline Burney, being desirous of carrying her brother's intentions into effect, generously renewed the offer.

The Prize is to be awarded to a Graduate of the University, who is not of more than three years' standing from admission to his first Degree when the Essays are sent in, and who shall produce the best English Essay "on some moral or metaphysical subject, on the Existence, Nature, and Attributes of God, or on the Truth and Evidence of the Christian Religion." The successful Candidate is required to print his Essay; and after having delivered, or caused to be delivered, a copy of it to the University Library, the Library of Christ's College, the University Libraries of Oxford, Dublin, and Edinburgh, and to each of the Adjudicators of the Prize, he is to receive from the Vice-Chancellor the year's interest of the Stock, from which sum the Candidate is to pay the expenses of printing the Essay.

The Vice-Chancellor, the Master of Christ's College, and the Norrisian Professor of Divinity, are the Examiners of the Compositions and the Adjudicators of the Prize.

THE ETHICAL AND SOCIAL ASPECT

OF

HABITUAL CONFESSION TO A PRIEST.

IN approaching the subject of Confession there is a preliminary difficulty which has seldom been taken sufficient account of. It has been common for those who have treated of the subject to argue as though there were an entire agreement with respect to the end which Confession has in view and as though its power of attaining this end were the only subject of dispute.

As a matter of fact, however, there is no such general agreement and consequently much that has been written for and against the Confessional has fallen wide of the mark. There are two entirely different views taken of the nature and object of Confession. By one class of persons it is regarded as aiming in common with other institutions at the progress and moral development of mankind, and is pronounced good or bad according as it is thought to aid or retard this progress. By another class again, it is regarded as having a special aim which distinguishes it from all other institutions: this aim being to realise a special promise made by Our Lord to His Apostles and through them to all duly qualified Ministers of His Church[1]. Confession on the one view acts according to the ordinary laws and conditions of progress and on the other has a special mode of action and leads to results which are not to be accounted for on the general principles of human nature.

These different views of the object of Confession may obviously give occasion to two distinct and separate disputes. On the one hand those who

---

[1] The view of Confession here alluded to is what is called the "Sacramental" theory of Confession. For a fuller description of it see Appendix.

regard it as a purely human institution may dispute among themselves as to the good or bad which, as an institution, it is likely to effect : whether there are any conditions under which it may do useful work, and if so, whether they are such as are likely to be fulfilled at the present day. On the other hand, issue may be joined on the question whether there are sufficient grounds for the belief that Confession when followed by Absolution has the effects sometimes ascribed to it: whether again, there is any scriptural authority for the doctrine of the "Power of the Keys" and whether the "Apostolical Succession" can be made out in favour of the Clergy of the Church of England.

The mode of attack and defence in this case will be essentially different from that employed in the former dispute.

It will consist mainly in the examination of texts to see if they will bear the meaning which has been put upon them, in the comparison of different passages, the citation of authorities and appeals to history. With all this we shall have nothing to do in the present essay which is concerned only with the ethical and social aspect of Confession, but it is important to make it clear at the outset that there are two ways in which the subject may be treated, as much confusion has resulted from neglecting to distinguish between them. The Confessional has frequently been attacked on one set of principles and defended on another, and then disputants have been surprised to find that arguments which seemed convincing to themselves have had little or no effect on those against whom they were directed.

It has been thought strange, for example, that men who have been got to admit that the political and social tendencies of Confession may be hurtful, have yet been found to go on recommending the practice. But supposing them to be adherents to what is called the "Sacramental" theory of Confession, there is nothing to be wondered at in this. In this view Confession is a thing of divine appointment, having a different object from any other institution (for whatever else we may take to be the object of Government, for example, we cannot suppose it to aim at forgiveness of sins). Having different ends we have no means of deciding on the relative worth of The Confessional and Government. To try to compare them would be to attempt a comparison of incommensurables, and where the two institutions are found to conflict it is only natural to give the preference to the divine over the human. No amount of mere political or social harm, it will be said, can justify us in rejecting a means of salvation held out to us by God Himself and in neglecting to avail ourselves of His richest promises.

In short it is useless to attempt to reason such a one out of his advocacy of Confession by any demonstration of tendencies or results. So long as he retains his belief in its divine origin he will be unaffected by anything that can be said on this head. The only line of argument that will be likely to lead to any result with such a man will be that which aims at showing the insufficiency of the ground on which his belief in Confession as a divine institution is based. If it can be proved that there is nothing in the Bible to countenance such a theory and that the whole doctrine of the "Power of the Keys" is based on a misconception, the opponent of Confession may not unreasonably hope to convince his adversary, but nothing short of this will be likely to have any effect except to embitter the dispute and widen the gulf between them.

We shall have nothing to say then, in the present essay, to those who maintain that Confession is a divine institution standing on a different footing from all others and to be judged by principles peculiar to itself. We shall view it throughout as a purely human means of assisting mankind in the struggle towards perfection and endeavour to ascertain whether at the present day it is more likely to aid or retard their progress in this direction.

In weighing the evidence for and against the practice it will be necessary to take into account the effect which Confession will be likely to have on the different forms of intercourse between men which go by the name of "social institutions." It is here that the "social aspect" of Confession will come to be considered, and the opinion we form of it will have an important influence in determining the general result.

It not unfrequently happens that an institution, which, if it stood alone, might be productive of good results, is entirely unfit for adoption because of the injury it will do to other institutions. The indirect harm it will thus occasion may more than outweigh the good, which in its own nature it is calculated to produce.

Progress, it must be remembered, is the result of the combined action of many causes, and in order that any new institution may be of use, it is essential that it should act in harmony with those which already exist. Now in order to judge by its probable effect on the rest (as well as by its direct influence on character) whether Confession may fairly claim to have a place among the institutions of our time, we must first have a clear idea of the laws and conditions of that progress which we have assumed to be the end and object of all.

For it must be borne in mind that human beings are subject to law in the moral as well as in the material world. This fact, which is really implied in the existence of every institution having a moral aim, is one which many persons (especially those who claim to be religious) are extremely reluctant to admit. They shrink from allowing the existence of a law of progress lest it should seem to exclude the operation of man's free will.

A moment's reflection ought to show, however, that there is no real inconsistency between the two, and that "free will" is not denied because it is maintained that there are many things which men cannot do without the use of means or without conformity to laws. God Himself, so far as it is permitted us to view His action, makes use of means to effect His purposes, and what is good in Him cannot be degrading in us. The material universe with its countless forms of beauty is built up by the combination and interaction of simple forces, each acting according to a fixed and unchanging law. There are said to be but sixty original substances out of which are compounded the infinite variety of natural objects which meet our eyes, and it is in the marvellous use made of these comparatively simple means that we find the surest proof of the existence of a Divine Ruler of the universe and of a moral purpose which He is ever engaged in working out.

Since, then, progress is possible only to those who act in conformity with fixed laws, we must set ourselves to discover what these laws are before we can undertake to judge of the value of any particular institution. Having made ourselves acquainted with the general principles of moral progress and the conditions under which institutions may render useful service, we must next proceed to examine whether these conditions are likely to be fulfilled in the particular case of Confession, which we must pronounce to be good or bad according to the result of the examination.

By thus treating the subject in a philosophic

spirit, and working our way upwards from fundamental principles of human nature, we are more likely, it is thought, to arrive at a satisfactory conclusion than if we were to follow the usual method of simply collecting together the arguments for and against the Confessional, and arraying the one set against the other. Such a method indeed, is hardly open to us here, our concern being with ethical and social principles as they apply to the subject of Confession, and apart from its unphilosophical character there are other obvious objections to be urged against it.

To commence, then, with our explanation of moral progress:—

Man is a being possessed of various impulses, desires and affections, all prompting him to action and gaining strength in proportion to the amount of action they give occasion to.

Among these desires is one which may be most appropriately described as the Love of Duty, the nature and office of which is to lead men to do what they believe to be morally right. This desire is one which is never wholly extinguished even in the most degraded[1], though it is found to exist in varying degrees of strength according to the amount of exercise afforded it.

It constitutes the moral part of our nature, the possession of which distinguishes man from the rest of created beings.

It is in the strengthening and development of this desire to do what is right and good, that all moral progress consists, and the end to which all progress is slowly tending is its absolute and undisputed supremacy over the meaner impulses of our nature.

When magnified to infinity and acting in harmony with infinite wisdom it affords the highest conception which men can frame of the attributes of the Deity Himself.

[1] Cf. Kant, *Metaph. of Ethics*, Bk. iv. 12, "We have an original susceptibility for having our free choice impelled by pure practical reason and her law, and this it is which is termed the moral feeling." "No man is destitute of this feeling, and were he deprived of all capacity for being thus affected he would be ethically dead." See also Sidgwick's *Methods of Ethics*, Bk. I., chap. 3, "There exists in all moral agents as such a permanent desire (varying no doubt very much in strength from time to time and in different persons), to do what is right and reasonable because it is such."

In highest wisdom guiding perfect love of right we recognise the divine ideal towards which it is man's privilege to struggle, however far short of it he may be destined to fall.

If moral goodness, then, is summed up in the development and strengthening of the love of duty, in what sense—it will be natural to ask—are other motives such as love of justice, benevolence, charity, &c. spoken of as good; and again how far are we justified in ascribing rightness of a certain sort to the natural impulses which tend to the satisfaction of bodily wants?

How do all these stand related to the love of duty, and, in cases where they are found to conflict with each other, on what principles are we to decide between them? These are questions which have called forth a variety of answers from different Schools of moralists and which must be settled one way or another before any satisfactory notion of moral progress can be formed.

The true explanation, as it seems to us, is simply this.—The love of duty like all other motives gains strength by being acted upon, and action for duty implies resistance of all motives which prompt to a different course. Other motives, therefore, are useful as supplying the *material* for the love of duty to work upon. They are good only so far as by being overcome they give strength to the motive (love of duty) which has subdued them. As death in nature is the condition of new life, and the seed must decay in the ground before the flower can spring up; so in the moral world it is only by the sacrifice of their own life that the non-moral motives can *directly* aid the moral.

In this resistance of other motives, however, as a means of gaining strength, the love of duty must not choose its opponents blindly.

If, without calculating its strength, it sets itself to overcome some strong impulse (as an appetite which long indulgence has made powerful), it will run the risk of failure, and increased weakness instead of strength will be the result. For, on the same principle that success strengthens, defeat leads to loss of strength. The love of duty, therefore, must be content to develope itself gradually, never risking defeat by attempting what is clearly beyond its power, and always ready, when necessary, to avail itself of those means and aids which reason and experience suggest.

These means consist in the adjustment and combination of the non-moral motives (*i.e.*, all motives except love of duty), so that in resisting any one of them, the love of duty will not only have its own strength to rely upon, but will be backed and supported by that of another motive.

Thus it will call out love of industry to aid (*indirectly*) in its conflict with idleness, and self-respect to contend with debasing passions, while sympathy and family affections will be cultivated to assist duty in its hardest task, that of overcoming the exaggerated love of self which is the source of so much of the world's evil and misery. The strength gained by the resulting conquest in any of these cases may enable love of duty to attempt the next resistance by its own unaided force and so to develope itself still more. For it must be remembered that it is only by what it does itself that the love of duty can gather strength. Other motives may prepare the field of action for it but they cannot act for it. They must be pronounced bad in all cases where they give their assistance when there is no absolute need for it (as the opportunity for duty to act and strengthen itself is thereby taken away) and good only when they hold in check some too-powerful motive which love of duty wants strength to oppose directly.

There are many motives which are so frequently employed by love of duty to aid in resisting others, that they have come to be regarded as having an absolute worth of their own, though in reality they are good only as *means* and their aid would not be required in a state of ideal perfection. Such are justice, benevolence, patriotism, &c. and as, in the present state of the world, there is never a sufficiency of these motives to aid duty in resisting the lower impulses and in keeping the passions and appetites within due bounds, many motives are encouraged solely on the ground that they assist in strengthening justice, &c. by helping them to resist their opponents. Fear of punishment, for example, is employed as an aid to love of justice which is itself one of the most valuable aids to love of duty. In the same way a habit of attending to religious forms and observances is cultivated as a means of awaking reverence and true religious feeling which are among duty's most powerful allies. Thus we have an ascending scale of motives culminating in love of duty, each of which derives what moral worth it has from the degree in which it directly or indirectly aids this latter motive in strengthening itself.

Now this adjusting of motives by love of duty to further its own growth and development by making its conquests gradual and sure, is not a work which each man can perform only for himself. On the contrary it is one which requires for its fullest efficiency the cooperation of all mankind, and everything which tends to draw men together and promote harmony of action between them has a share in the furtherance of this work. When one man is in danger of having his love of duty overpowered by the force of an inferior motive, others may come to his assistance and call out by precept or example some aid-motive which he himself has lost through ignorance or neglect the power to summon up. Thus the sense of self-respect may have lost its deterring power under the influence of degrading habits and may be called back to life and vigour by the remonstrances and pleadings of a friend. Or an affection which has long lain dormant may be rekindled by a friendly hand, and exert once more its purifying influence on the heart. By repressing here and encouraging there the desires and impulses which retard or aid it, the course of moral progress may be hastened in a thousand different ways and the work of duty made more and more equal to the capacity of all men.

Reason and experience alone can guide us in determining the precise place and time in which this assistance is required, but, wherever and whenever it is called for, the manner of its action will be in all cases alike, and until we were acquainted with this we could not have judged fairly of any of the forms which it has been made to assume. For every institution, whether political, social, moral or religious, is but a special form in which this assistance is realised, and is to be pronounced good or bad on the principles we have just laid down.

Government, for example, is an institution having for its special object the security of life and property, which effects its purposes by a system of commands and prohibitions the sum of which constitutes *Law*. Its moral value is to be measured (as in all other cases) by the degree in which it aids the love of duty in resisting and conquering other motives. By opposing the fear of punishment to the promptings of idleness and passion it causes these latter gradually to die out and give place to the desires and tastes which belong to a state of settled order. Respect for human life and love of industry and peaceful pursuits become in time the prevailing motives, and in proportion as these are more conducive to moral progress and the development of the love of duty, so is Government to be accounted superior to the state of disorder which preceded it.

All other institutions in a similar way have special ends in view by which their value is commonly judged of, but, if we wish to ascertain their ethical worth as aids to progress, we must look beyond these immediate results and see how far the dispositions and desires which flow from them are likely to prove valuable allies to the love of duty.

Having now seen how it is that qualities and motives (and institutions founded upon them) which have no absolute value of their own, can yet be made to assist in the work of moral progress, or, in other words, in the developing and strengthening of the love of duty which alone is absolutely good; we are in a position to return to Confession and examine whether on the principles just laid down it is likely or not to render useful service.

And here in the first place it may be remarked that what has been said above of the nature and objects of institutions in general disposes at once of an objection which has sometimes been brought against Confession, viz. that it must be bad, because it is a means of getting that done for you which you would be better if you did for yourself. This, it will now be seen, is an objection which might be urged with equal force against every institution that has ever existed, whether political, social, or religious.

There is not one of them which does not owe its existence to the fact that men are not what they should be and which would not cease to be needed if they should ever reach perfection.

It would be better no doubt that a man should stand by his own unaided strength and work out his own salvation for himself, than that he should have to rely on another's help; but, on the other hand, it is better that he should rise by the help of others than that he should never rise at all. Institutions are made for men as they are found to exist and not as it is conceivable that they might be, and it would be the height of folly to reject what is useful now, because under a different set of circumstances it might be better to be without it.

The true question to ask is, not, Would mankind be better if they did for themselves what the institution we are examining attempts to do for them? (to which question there can be but one answer)—but, Will they be likely under existing circumstances to do this for themselves; or, in other words, will Confession be likely to supersede self-action and self-reliance or will it only assist those who would not otherwise make any progress at all?

This is the first great question by the answer to which we must form our opinion of Confession. There are three others of nearly equal importance which it may be well to notice shortly here as they will form together with the one just given the four main heads under which the arguments against Confession will be ranged. The second question, then, by which the Confessional must be tried, is, Will its tendency be to enable those who resort to it to dispense gradually with its aid? Will it be regarded as serving a *temporary* purpose, and its guidance and counsel as being justifiable only so far as it leads men to act and think for themselves? Unless these conditions are complied with the institution must be condemned, as indeed must all others. Progress implies perpetual change and no institution can be good which aims at keeping things as they are. This is a truth which, obvious as it seems, men are even now very apt to forget. It is not so common a thing as it once was to hear politicians disputing about the "best form of government," and reasoning as though the precise constitution needed for a particular country could be determined on "a priori" principles; but the old notion still lingers on, and theologians have been among the very last to shake themselves free from its influence, and admit that institutions must in all cases depend for their value upon conditions of time and place.

The third great question to be asked with respect to Confession is—Will it be regarded and employed as a means only to moral progress, and not as a thing good in itself and possessed of some peculiar sanctity of its own?

Under this head we shall have to take account, not only of the natural tendency, which all moralists notice, to invest with the importance of *ends* things which have been found useful as *means*, but of the special danger of this mistake being made, which the prevalence of the "Sacramental" theory of Confession will be likely to occasion. This theory of the nature and object of Confession will naturally have its effect on the character and opinions of those who have adopted it. Its existence can generally be traced by the exaggerated importance given to such acts as introspection and self-examination which will always be found to rank higher where confession is regarded as an end in itself than where its effect on progress is all that is looked to.

There is a certain set of opinions, in short, which are the natural and logical result of the view of Confession here alluded to, and this part of our enquiry will be mainly taken up in ascertaining the extent to which they prevail among the modern advocates of the practice, and their importance and value in an ethical point of view.

The fourth and last question we shall have to ask will relate to the "social" aspect of the subject, which will only have been indirectly touched upon before.

We shall have to enquire into the effect which Confession will be likely to have on the different forms of intercourse between men which constitute what is known as "social life."

As each of these possesses a distinct ethical value of its own, it will be necessary to ascertain in what this consists and how far there is reason to think it will be impaired by the revival of Confession, before we can be in a position to pronounce our final judgment.

These, then, are the four main questions to which a satisfactory answer must be given before the practice of Confession can be made out to be a beneficial one.

They afford no arbitrary test, but are questions by which the worth of any institution might be tried. It has been our aim throughout this essay to bring the subject of Confession under the operation of universal principles of morality, and if this method has led us at times to discuss ethical rules at what may seem undue length, our justification must be that the subject has hitherto been treated with far too little regard to general principles. Some writers seem to have taken it for granted that the end and object of Confession must be familiar to all, and that therefore no explanation on that head could be needed. Hence has arisen the confusion which was pointed out in the opening pages of this essay.

Again much that has been written on this subject has been rendered practically worthless through ignorance on the part of the writers of the nature and office of institutions and the conditions under which they work. Others again have treated of Confession as though it were the only institution existing or as though its influence upon others were a thing not worth taking account of.

All this has made it important that in dealing

with the ethical and social aspect of Confession we should proceed with great caution : clearing the ground as we go on of erroneous and misleading views, and only entering on the detailed examination of the subject when a secure foundation has been laid for it in general principles.

Enough has now been said to enable us to appreciate the ethical value of the facts and arguments which may be produced for and against the practice of Confession. In dealing with these it will be well to consider first those good effects which, in our opinion, may be expected from it. No institution it is probable has ever produced unmixed evil and we are willing to allow many possible benefits to the institution of Confession. These good results however are balanced (and more than balanced) by serious evils, the consideration of which occupy the greater number of the remaining pages of this essay. They will be treated of under four main heads, as they follow from an unsatisfactory answer being obliged to be given to the four great questions laid down above.

To begin then with the good side of Confession and consider what may fairly be urged in its favour. There is an infinite variety of ways in which the strong can aid the weak, and the erring and sinful be led back to the path of duty, and induced once more to take up the divine work of progress from which they have turned aside. The conditions which must be observed in rendering this assistance have already been pointed out, and it would be most unfair to assume that they will in all cases be neglected by those who are charged with hearing Confessions. When we maintain that the tendency of Confession will be to weaken the inward power of Conscience and Will, and to encourage an undue reliance on external aids, we do not mean to say that such will inevitably and in all cases be the result. There have been men in past times, and we cannot doubt that they have their equals at the present day, in whose hands the Confessional has been a powerful influence for good. Taking a true view of its nature as a human institution and having no selfish interests of their own to serve, they have made it their chief endeavour to shame men out of their selfishness and indifference, and rouse in them something of that moral energy without which repentance must ever be an empty mockery. Far from seeking to exalt their own influence and maintain their hold on the consciences and wills of those who have come to them for aid, they have striven to render such assistance unnecessary in the future by calling back into activity and life the powers that have lain neglected within.

It is only a spirit of blind opposition which refuses to view a question in any light but one; that can affect to deny that good may thus be done through the medium of the Confessional. We, who are anxious to regard the matter in a broader and more liberal spirit, doing justice to every side of it, are ready to make the fullest admission of this, and we can afford to do so without in any way endangering the general position which we have taken up. We can even go further and allow that there are evils arising out of the circumstances and conditions of the present day which Confession is fitted in a special manner to meet and correct.

Indifference and neglect of religious matters prevail among us to an extent which is exciting not unreasonable alarm. Religion, it is to be feared, is exerting less and less control over the life and thought of average Englishmen, and material or, as it is sometimes called, "practical" good is becoming more and more the engrossing object of pursuit.

It is no new thing, it is true, for irreligion and worldliness to show themselves in England, but it has usually been among the higher strata of Society that their effects have been most remarked. The noticeable thing at the present day is the alarming rate at which indifference to religious wants is making its way among the lowest classes who have hitherto escaped the contagion.

Another evil peculiar to our times is the growing separation of classes. There is less intercourse and therefore less sympathy between the rich and the poor, the educated and the ignorant, than at any former time. Charitable institutions, it is true, are as abundant and flourishing as ever, but, for the most part, they do very little to bring men of different classes together, and can never be made to supply the place of individual aid and sympathy.

This separation of classes has been accounted for in a variety of ways, but, whatever may be taken to be its true cause, the evil itself must be admitted to be a serious one.

Now Confession if judiciously employed may do something to meet both these evils.

On the one hand, by the impressive nature of the ceremony, and by the direct individual action which it involves, it may be expected to have an effect in drawing attention to spiritual needs which no amount of general exhortations or public observances would be likely to produce.

The fact, on the other hand, of there being persons specially appointed to receive Confessions and administer sympathy and advice, may in some measure supply the place of that sympathetic intercourse in which our age is felt to be deficient.

Many men, who might be held back by natural shyness or timidity from applying to an ordinary acquaintance for counsel in spiritual matters, may be glad to seek help from one with whom they may be sure at least of attention and secrecy, and who, from special training and experience, may be expected to give real assistance. The hardening effects of hidden and unrepented sin: the despair which comes from an unsuccessful effort at reform, and leads to recklessness and indifference—the perplexity and needless self-torment to which those are often reduced who are left to grapple alone with their doubts:—all these things, on which the advocates of Confession insist so strongly, are real practical evils which we cannot afford to neglect, and we should not be acting fairly to our opponents if we were to ignore the effect which Confession may possibly have in removing them.

By refusing to take account of facts like these, or appearing to make light of them and explain them away, we should only be giving colour to the complaint which has been so frequently made by the defenders of the Confessional that they have never had justice done them, or their cause allowed a fair hearing.

While however we are willing to give them the full benefit of these admissions, we do not attach by any means the same importance to them as our opponents, who seem to think that a judgment in favour of Confession can hardly fail to follow from them. There are many people who imagine that they have proved their case and done all that can be required of them when they have succeeded in bringing forward one or two plausible arguments in support of it. Other things, however, may require to be done, and other sides of the question to be heard, before they can be in a position to call for judgment. The fact that there are strong arguments in favour of Confession does not prevent there being stronger arguments against it, and this we shall presently see to be the case. It is not enough to show that there are circumstances and conditions under which Confession may do useful work, and that there are men existing who might be trusted to observe these conditions. This is all very well as far as it goes, but unfortunately it goes only a very little way.

The further and more practical question still remains,—Will these conditions be likely to be fulfilled in the majority of cases and by the majority of Confessors at the present day, or, in other words, will the *general tendency* of the institution be likely to be good rather than bad?

We must be prepared to answer "yes" or "no" to this question, and must be careful not to let ourselves be led away from it by imagining what Confession might be in an exceptional state of things or in the hands of exceptional people.

We might agree, to take a parallel case, that Representative Government is a higher and more advanced form of Government than a Despotism of any kind, and yet hesitate very reasonably before pronouncing it fit for adoption in India at the present day; even though we could point to instances of natives having attained a degree of culture more than sufficient to fit them for the exercise of freedom. The general tendency, in short, is what we must look to in all such cases, and in computing this we must take men as we find them and not as we choose to fancy that they might be.

If, indeed, Confession were a thing which, if it did not effect the good expected from it, would simply leave things as they were before, a very small amount of probable good would justify us in giving it a trial; but this is by no means the case.

Where it does not do good, Confession is certain to do positive harm. If it does not further progress, it will retard it and put fresh obstacles in the path of duty.

The extent to which it is likely to do so is what we are now called upon to consider, and, in pursuance of the plan laid down above, we shall first consider the bad results which may be expected to follow from the fact of Confession *doing for men what they would otherwise do for themselves* (or, in other words, from the probable injury that will be done to habits of self-reliance).

Now, in the first place, no reasonable person can doubt that the counsel and guidance of a Confessor will he asked for and received in many cases where the person soliciting it is perfectly competent to act and think for himself: where his conscience could tell him all that is required, if he would only give it the chance, and where nothing but an exercise of will which is quite within his power is needed to give effect to its decision. In such cases, and any one who has been at the pains to enquire into the sort of communications which ordinarily pass between Confessor and penitent will know them to be common enough, Confession does nothing but unmitigated harm. It simply becomes a means of shirking responsibility and purchasing ease and freedom from anxiety by a surrender of the conscience and will; a direct loss of moral strength being the necessary and unavoidable result. It is found to be less trouble to let another resolve your doubts and set out your tasks for you than to wrestle with and overcome them for yourself and so increase and develop the powers which were given you for the purpose.

The love of duty (on which we saw moral progress to be based) gains strength in proportion to the acts of duty it gives rise to, and how can it be expected to increase when all that you have done for it has been to take your cares and anxieties and throwing them at the feet of another ask him to do for you what you are too lazy to do for yourself[1]?

Again, it is not the wilfully idle and wilfully ignorant alone who will thus make an injurious use of the Confessional, else there would always be a chance of their being detected and sent back by a conscientious and discerning Confessor. Men are

[1] *Four Cardinal Virtues*, by Rev. Orby Shipley, Sermon 2.
"The only advice which I will give is this: take these difficulties to your director; ask his judgment upon them; and be guided by his decision."
Again, Bp Wilberforce: "It (Confession) is nothing short of the renunciation of the great charge of a conscience which God has committed to every man."
Again, Dr Pusey himself says, "I wish something could be done to check the tendency on the part of some clergy to claim implicit obedience on all sorts of subjects from their penitents."

strangely apt to be deceived in their estimate of their own strength, and seldom know how much it is in their power to accomplish. They rarely err in attempting too much, but are easily led to think themselves weaker than they really are. If they see assistance offered they will readily persuade themselves that they require its aid and cannot get along without it, and this tendency will naturally be strengthened wherever the "sacramental" theory retains any influence and Confession is regarded as having a mysterious and superhuman efficacy. To teach men that they are weak is a sure way to make them so, and there is always danger lest an institution of this sort should create the wants it is designed to satisfy.

That this is no imaginary danger in the case of Confession will readily be allowed by all who have studied the working of the institution in countries where it has been long in use. Nor is it a sufficient answer to say that the priest may be trusted to check this tendency and give his aid only when there is real need for it. For, even assuming him to be above all temptation to abuse his power and anxious only to do his best for all who apply to him, how is he to know whether or not a man is deceived in his estimate of his own character and powers? He can only give useful advice so far as he is acquainted with the condition of his patients, and for this he will be obliged to rely in the great majority of cases simply and solely on what they themselves are able to tell him. For priests, though they are not unfrequently in danger of forgetting it, are after all but ordinary human beings, possessed of like faculties with the rest of mankind, and in no way gifted beyond others in the special power of reading character;—unless, indeed, we choose to credit them with the "Power of the Keys," and take it to imply a prophetic insight into character—(an interpretation which it will bear quite as readily as the one more commonly put upon it[1]).

---

[1] Bishop Hall maintains that there are two "Keys," and credits the English clergy with the possession of both.

"Doubtless every true minister of Christ hath, by virtue of this first and everlasting commission, two keys delivered into his hands: the *Key of Knowledge* and the *Key of Spiritual Power:* the one whereby he is enabled to enter and search into, not only the revealed

Special training may do something no doubt in helping men to form judgments of character, but it is absurd to expect that it will really enable one man to know another better than he knows himself, and unless it can do this—and not in a few cases only but generally—the objection we are urging remains unanswered. If then under the most favorable conditions, and supposing there to be a sincere desire to do what is right on the part of both priest and penitent, there is danger of Confession being thus abused, how much greater must this danger be when any of these conditions are wanting! We cannot affect to think that all Confessors will in all cases resist the numerous temptations which beset them[1] (the temptation, for

mysteries of salvation, but also in some sort *into the heart of the penitent*, &c." (*Resolutions and Decisions of divers practical cases of Conscience*, Case IX.)

[1] How great the temptations and difficulties in the way of a Confessor are likely to be may be judged by the following quotations from the Abbé Gaume's *Manual for Confessors* (translated by Dr Pusey for Anglican use).

" Practically the office of a Confessor, which seems so easy, is *most difficult*. It binds you to three things: 1. To acquire a high moral tone as *judge* and great skill as *physician*. 2. To use both carefully for the penitent's welfare. 3. To take upon yourself a example, to increase their own influence and importance, or to save themselves trouble by a speedy absolution), or that all will escape the influence of the doctrine which claims for the Clergy a sanctity beyond the reach of the rest of mankind. And yet, wherever one or other of these temptations is yielded to, the probability of Confession doing harm instead of good will be indefinitely increased and a weakening of conscience and will cannot fail to be the result.

An answer has been given to the objection just

great deal of labor so that the wandering sheep may not be tempted to hate both fold and shepherd and fly both for ever."

"The Confessor who has only a father's charity without the judge's knowledge and the physician's skill, may wish to succour souls but will not know how to do so."

"The ministry of Confession requires *constant mortification* and setting aside occupations and pursuits more to your taste, in order to fulfil the office which is *at once wearisome to the body and full of anxiety* both as to your own soul and to those of your penitents."

"Seek detachment from all things; friends, property, pleasures; else the love of the world will soon draw you from the road to Heaven."

The Abbé also remarks, "The experience of many years has taught me that a great number of Confessors have an extreme inclination to give absolution on the spot without examining the state of the penitent;" and goes on to say, "perhaps out of four score persons plunged in habitual sin more than three score and ten have been lost through these ignorant and lukewarm Confessors."

urged against Confession, that it will be likely to supersede self-action and lead therefore to decline of moral strength, which it may be well to notice and comment on here. This particular objection has been met by a simple denial that the practice of relying on the guidance of a spiritual adviser implies weakness of any kind.

The "iron characters" which the Church of Rome has in all ages produced are appealed to in proof of this. How, it is triumphantly asked, can an institution which has aided in forming the characters of so many saints and martyrs be accused of promoting weakness? Now this argument, which seems at first sight to have a good deal of plausibility in it, is not one which need give us any great amount of trouble, but it is worthy of attention from the influence which it undoubtedly exerts. We have no need to deny or attempt to lessen in any way the force of the facts on which it is based, but may content ourselves with simply denying the inference which it is attempted to draw from them.

Granted that among those who have been

trained by the Confessional there have been men of the highest courage; men who have been ready to face all dangers and have not even shrunk from death itself when it met them in the path of duty; all this does not in the least affect what we have said of the tendency of Confession to encourage an undue reliance on others and thereby weaken the force of conscience and will.

On the contrary these examples tend rather to confirm than disprove our statement, for, whatever their virtues, it has never been maintained that these Catholic saints and heroes were remarkable for *independence* either of thought or action. Their steady obedience to authority and meek acceptance of the doctrines laid down for them were counted among their highest claims to honor, and it is here rather than in the nobler sides of their character that the influence of the Confessional is to be traced. They would have gained a very different reputation from that of Saints if they had presumed to take moral progress as their ideal and aimed at independence and self-relying strength. Unless they had submitted to be guided by authority and consented to act as the instruments of another's will, their virtues would have availed little to save them from a heretic's fate.

There may be much to honour and admire in the character of such men, but the type which they represent is far from being the highest humanity can reach, and it is absurd to cite as examples of moral strength men whose whole life was spent in reliance on external authority. There is, it is true, a strength of a certain sort which is compatible with and often increased by the completest dependence on others; but it is the strength of unreflecting ignorance: the strength of enthusiasts and fanatics, and not that of a properly developed man[1].

---

[1] Cf. Kant, *Metaph. of Ethics*, Bk. IV. 2, "By strength of soul we understand the steadfastness of a man's will, as a being endowed with freedom, i.e. in so far as he is in a healthy state of intellect and retains his command over himself." And again, "In fine, this sort of question may be compared to the question whether a person may not have greater physical power in a fit of phrenzy than when he is in his right wits; and this question may be answered in the affirmative without allowing him upon that account to be possessed of greater strength of soul."

By sacrificing one part of your nature, you may generally succeed in forcing another part to an abnormal degree of power (as we see in the unnatural physical strength which is said to accompany madness); and those who confine their view to the resulting strength, ignoring the price paid for it, may easily see nothing but good in the cause of such a state of things.

There are others, however, who are not satisfied with a partial view like this, and who think that the surrender of conscience and will implied in Roman Catholic saintliness is an aspect of the matter which is well worth taking account of. They hold that a man's faculties were given him to be used and developed and not to be handed over meekly to the keeping of others, and that the great bulk of mankind are fitted to be something better than tools—however serviceable, or slaves—

Again, Humboldt says (*Sphere v. Duties of Government*, p. 92), "It is true that where belief has stifled every form of doubt and gained the supreme mastery, it often creates a more irresistible courage and extraordinary spirit of defiant endurance, as we see in the history of all enthusiasts, but this kind of energy is *never desirable*," &c.

however devoted, at the disposal of a select and favored fraction of the race[1].

If then the plea has to be rejected that dependence on others does not imply loss of moral strength, the advocates of Confession have to fall back again upon the argument that as a matter of fact it will not be found to encourage an undue reliance on others, but will be employed only in cases where it is acknowledged that guidance and assistance are needed. The fact that they have been obliged to resort to such a plea as that just noticed shews that they are not very confident

---

[1] The defenders of Confession are fond of quoting Jeremy Taylor, let us therefore hear what he has to say on this subject: "It is best to follow our guides if we know nothing better, but if we do it is better to follow the pillar of fire than the pillar of cloud, though both possibly may lead to Canaan."

" If without the particular engagement of my own understanding I follow a guide, possibly I may be guilty of extreme negligence, or I may extinguish God's spirit, or do violence to my own reason. And whether intrusting myself wholly with another be not a laying up my talent in a napkin, I am not so well assured."

"It is commanded as a duty 'of ourselves to be able to judge what is right,' 'to try all things and retain that which is best.'"
" For he that resolves not to consider resolves not to be careful whether he hath truth or no, and therefore hath an affection indifferent to truth, which is all one as if he did choose amiss."

of success in this quarter and have an uneasy suspicion that the facts are against them. There are other indications too that they would like if possible to shift their ground and find some easier task than that of directly meeting the charge that Confession will be resorted to when there is no real need for it.

Mr Carter tries to evade the difficulty by the assertion that the evils of over direction result only from the *abuse* of Confession and have no *necessary* connection with the practice[1]. This is perfectly true, no doubt, and would be a fit answer to a charge of directly aiming at these evils. But what we are urging here is not that these results are intended, but that as a matter of fact they will be found to follow. If it can be shewn that practically an institution works badly and produces bad results, it is a very poor excuse to say that its promoters

[1] "The evils popularly associated with the idea of direction and ordinarily intended to be condemned under the term, viz., the substitution of the priest's judgment for the true acting of the conscience of the person under his influence and the consequent loss of all sense of obligation of personal responsibility, *are but the abuse of a most sacred trust.*" *The Doctrine of Confession*, Chap. XIV.

intended it to do something different. We are willing to give the advocates of Confession credit for meaning well, and have already conceded that there are conceivable conditions under which it might do good service, but what we maintain is that these conditions will not be observed in the great majority of cases, and that under existing circumstances the institution is certain to be abused in the manner pointed out above.

Another way of escape is open to those who take the view that the object of Confession is not to aid moral progress, but to get the benefit of absolution which priests have at their disposal by divine grant and favor.

They can afford to admit in the most ample way the danger of "over direction," as the strength of their position is no way affected by it. Dr Pusey, for example, lays great stress on the harm done by the claim to implicit obedience put forward by many Confessors[1].

---

[1] "I wish something could be done to check the tendency on the part of some clergy to claim *implicit obedience* on all sorts of subjects

Dr Neale goes further, and condemns all "direction" whatever, not only as of dangerous tendency but as inconsistent with the real object of Confession[1]. This is reasonable enough from the point of view of the believers in the miraculous efficacy of the "power of the Keys," but those defenders of Confession with whom alone we have any direct concern in this essay (those, viz., who regard it as a means of aiding moral progress), obviously cannot avail themselves of this theory as a means of escape. If Confession, in their view, does any good at all, it can only be by the guidance or direction which it affords, and all that Dr Pusey and others say of the dangers of "over direction" must tell with fatal effect upon their position.

from their penitents." (Introduction to Dr Pusey's translation of the Abbé Gaume's work on Confession.)

[1] "Nothing can be more important than to set prominently before English Churchmen the fact that with "Direction of this kind, Confession has no necessary connection whatever."

"Plainly any who use Confession for advice rather than for *absolution* should be sent back." "We know how many, especially among women, in coming to Confession for the first time, come rather for *direction* than for *absolution:* look for the *guide* rather than for the *ambassador;* desire the *counsellor* rather than the *priest.*"

Enough has now been said of the liability of Confession to overstep the limits, within which alone it can do good, and to retard moral progress by its weakening influence on the conscience and will.

We now pass to the second of the four great heads into which the subject has been divided, and have to decide whether the tendency of Confession will or will not be to enable those who resort to it to dispense gradually with its aid, or, in other words, whether or not it will be regarded and employed as a *temporary* discipline by which men are to be trained to act and think for themselves.

Unless a favorable answer can be given to this question, Confession must be condemned (in accordance with the principles laid down above when we were discussing the nature and value of institutions) and we maintain and shall attempt to prove that with respect to the great majority of cases the answer will not be a favorable one.

So far from tending to diminish the need for assistance, this is almost invariably found to increase in proportion to the length of time that the Confessional has been established. This result has over and over again been pointed out and has suggested a comparison with drugs which, like opium, require to be taken more and more frequently and in ever-increasing quantities in order to produce their due effect; and which end by becoming a dreaded but indispensable necessity.

The most satisfactory way of dealing with this part of our subject will be to bring forward in the first place one or two instances out of the many which might be produced in confirmation of the opinion just given, and then endeavour to account shortly for the tendency which they help to prove. The Abbé Gaume (in his Manual of Confession before alluded to) quotes the testimony of a notorious sinner in proof of the value of a Confessor's influence. "When I was young and confessed to Father Philip I never was guilty of mortal sin; but alas I had no sooner left him than I fell into the licentious life I have led ever since."

Now it is easy to see what is implied in this.

It shows that in the opinion of one of its leading advocates (whose book Dr Pusey has translated for the use of English Clergy) Confession is not to be valued as a means of giving a man strength to guide and control himself, or this case would never have been thought to reflect credit on the ministrations of "Father Philip."

If Confession is to be judged on the same principles as other institutions and to be held good in proportion as it enables men to dispense with its aid and fits them for self-government, this is about as clear a case of failure as could well be produced, and yet there can be no doubt that the Abbé Gaume cited it as a proof of the value and use of Confession and never dreamed that he was furnishing a strong argument against it.

There is only one other example which space will permit us to quote here in support of the assertion that Confession will not be regarded and employed as a mere temporary discipline. At a recent meeting of the Church Congress Mr Compton said in pleading for "Sisterhoods" that the longer women remained in them the more often they felt the necessity of confessing. He evidently took this to imply an increasingly sensitive conscience on the part of the Sisters, but Canon Hoare's interpretation was probably the correct one when he gave it as his opinion that the fact alluded to by Mr Compton was only a particular instance of the general tendency of Confession to create the need for itself.

We have now to look for an explanation of this tendency or in other words to discover why it is that resort to Confession so frequently becomes habitual.

It is partly we think to be accounted for on a deeply-rooted principle of human nature, and is probably also in part the result of the peculiar view of the end and object of Confession which is taken by the great majority of those who wish to revive the practice in England.

Bishop Butler in his Chapter on "Moral discipline" lays great stress on the principle that while "practical habits are formed and strengthened by repeated acts, passive impressions on the other hand grow weaker by being repeated upon us."

Now applying this to the matter before us, we can easily see that not only is the practice of resorting to the Confessional for aid one which is always in danger of becoming habitual, but that its good effect on the feelings and character of penitents (in which its worth as a moral agent must consist) is liable to undergo a constant proportionate weakening. The moral emotions awakened by the act of confessing will be found to lose their force and die out with ever-increasing rapidity and there will be need for a more and more frequent repetition of it in order to produce the desired effect[1].

Resort to Confession, again, will naturally tend to become more frequent where the "sacramental" theory of its nature and object prevails. According to that theory Confession is a means of obtaining divine forgiveness for offences in virtue of a special

[1] See also Abercrombie on the *Philosophy of the Moral Feelings*, Part II. p. 138 (4th Edition).

promise made to the Apostles and their successors. Absolution, not guidance, is the end aimed at, and, as a sin cannot be pardoned unless it is confessed, and is liable to be forgotten unless Confession is frequent, the more frequently you confess, the more secure you may reasonably feel that you are walking in the path of salvation. The great thing to be avoided is having a mortal sin unconfessed and unabsolved, everything else is of subordinate interest; praiseworthy perhaps, but not of absolute obligation :—this alone is essential!

Now those who take this view of Confession (and though seldom so nakedly stated it is one which widely prevails even at the present day) cannot consistently find fault with the tendency of Confession to perpetuate itself and become habitual[1]

---

[1] On the contrary it is commonly regarded with favor as affording a special ground of security, *e.g.* "L'experience prouve que plus on se confesse souvent, moins on pèche grievement." (*Dictionnaire de Religion.*)

Again, the Rev. Orby Shipley in enumerating certain points in which his hearers may have "sinned against perseverance" mentions as one of them 'Abandonment of Confession when once adopted.' (*Sermon on the virtue of Prudence,* p. 70.)

Again in "An Autobiography" in *The Church and the World,*

or see anything to resent as an imputation in the statement that it is therefore *not* a mere temporary institution fulfilling the conditions by which all human institutions must be judged.

If, however, they can be brought to concede this, they will have given another direct blow to those who have based their defence of Confession on the ground of its being a serviceable human institution. It is against these latter only (it can hardly be necessary to repeat) that we are arguing in these pages, but, as the two modes of defence (which may be called respectively the theological and the ethical) are often employed as though they mutually strengthened and confirmed each other, we are justified in calling attention to their real inconsistency and in making use of the one as a means of attacking the other.

Having now illustrated and endeavoured to account for the failure of Confession to comply with the *second* great condition which when con-

(1866), the following opinion is given:—"I believe it (Confession) can never be intermitted when once begun habitually, without the deprivation being seriously felt by the soul."

sidered as a human institution it is bound to satisfy, we will pass on to the third of these conditions and enquire how far this too is likely to be broken and Confession to be regarded as *an end in itself* instead of a *means to progress*.

The tendency which is so commonly noticed for men to invest *means*, which have been long employed, with the importance of *ends* is only an instance of the general "Law of Association" which plays so important a part in moral philosophy[1]. It is a tendency which requires to be carefully guarded against and constitutes one of the dangers to which all institutions are more or less exposed. We constantly see old forms and practices retained and reverently defended, out of which all life and meaning have long since passed. Institutions which have once done useful service are kept up long after they have lost, through altered circumstances, all power for good, and have become drags and hindrances instead of aids to

---

[1] Cf. Bain's *Mental Science* (p. 105, 3rd Edit.).
Mill's *Logic* (Logic of the *Moral* Sciences, Chap. II.).

progress. The error of the Pharisees, who made religion to consist in conformity to symbolic rites and ceremonies and gave little or no thought to the inner meaning which they were meant to embody, has often been repeated since and is probably as common now as ever. The extent to which we put faith in *externals* has been made a special ground of reproach against our age. We have been accused[1] of clinging to forms and neglecting the spirit which alone can give them worth, and there is but too much reason to fear that the accusation is a just one. All this should make us particularly careful to avoid introducing any new institution the purpose of which is not obvious to all, as in such cases the danger we are alluding to is especially to be feared.

Now the danger of Confession being regarded as a thing good in itself, and of its gradually taking the place of the affections and motives it was meant

---

[1] *E.g.* by Carlyle, Mill, Humboldt. The complaint which Butler made with respect to his own time was the opposite one that the forms and ceremonies of religion were unduly neglected. (See Appendix to the "Analogy.")

to stimulate, is one which under any circumstances would require to be taken account of, and it cannot fail to be greatly increased by the prevalence of the sacramental theory. The fact that many of the most influential supporters of Confession value it not as a means to moral progress but *for its own sake*, (as constituting together with absolution a channel of divine pardon and grace), may not unreasonably be expected to influence those who began by regarding it as a human institution only.

In order to judge of the extent to which this misconception is likely to prevail, and Confession therefore to be diverted from its legitimate purpose, we must turn our attention to the kind of advice and instruction which is commonly given by Confessors, and to the qualities and conduct which they especially aim at encouraging, and see whether these are or are not such as will naturally conduce to moral progress and development.

We shall find as the result of our enquiry that the qualities which a Confessor commonly seeks to call out by his advice and guidance are different in many respects from those which a moralist with progress towards perfection as his aim would wish to cultivate. This difference, which is partly of kind and partly of degree, can only be accounted for by supposing that Confession *for its own sake* (or as a means only to absolution) is the real end which the Confessionalists have in view, and that even those who profess to take moral progress as their aim are really influenced to a much greater extent than they would allow by the prevailing theory. For the advice which is uniformly given by Manuals of Confession is of a kind which is reasonable and useful enough on the assumption that the sacerdotal theory is the true one. We shall proceed to give illustrations in proof of this and if we are successful in shewing that on this assumption only can the teaching and influence of Confession be approved, we shall have given a sufficient answer to those who defend the practice on ethical grounds.

To begin with the most important and at the same time the most obvious instance,—all Manuals of Confession insist strongly on the necessity of *constant self-examination and introspection*. This is the first and most imperative of duties which they are never tired of inculcating[1].

Motives and thoughts must be probed and examined: an exact Inventory of all offences must be kept, and their whole inward state must be kept constantly before men's eyes[2].

---

[1] *E.g.* "Confession must be distinct, unshrinking and complete. The earnest effort of the penitent must be to detail *every thought, word or deed* which he can ever remember to have committed." (*Ministry of Consolation.*)

Again a Book entitled *Pardon through the Precious Blood*, contains twelve rules for Confession of which the sixth is "Neither any concealment of sins *which is the worst of sacrilege*" and the seventh, "To be most explicit in those sins which it is the greatest pain to own." For further illustrations, which are too numerous and lengthy to quote, cf. *Manual of Confession*, pp. 11—29.

Again the Rev. W. Gresley says, "Forgiveness is *conditional* upon the completeness of the Confession." (Hints for the first Confession, *Ordinance of Confession*, 1851.)

[2] " He said I was to divide my life into periods of seven years, and to recollect *every circumstance* that had taken place in each period." Evidence of Eliz. Shiers in Rev. A. Poole's case.

Again, it was openly stated by Mr Hatchard at the Plymouth meeting that a child was taken to Confession at twelve years of age, to confess sins committed at the age of seven.

Dr Dodsworth describes himself as being "in the habit of receiving Confessions both of men and women, of their *whole* lives in details as minute as any that can possibly be made to a Catholic

Now all this is reasonable enough, and indeed highly necessary, if absolution is the end aimed at; for you cannot be absolved of sins which you have not confessed, and Confession implies a clear recollection of the offence. Constant vigilance therefore is necessary to prevent an offence being passed over through forgetfulness or inattention and to avoid the danger of carrying about with you the burden of an unforgiven sin.

It is hardly possible, in fact, on this theory to pay too much attention to your inward condition, and self-consciousness and introspection will naturally be exalted into the first of virtues[1].

Their value, however, in an ethical point of view, as aids to moral progress, will be very differently estimated. It is only within narrow limits that they are capable of rendering useful service at all, and when unduly encouraged, they have not

priest," and he adds, "It is only right to say so far as I know, that Confession is required to *be at least as minute* when observed in the Established Church as it is in the Catholic Church."

[1] "Christian life, according to the view of Confessors, as it approaches towards perfection will become more and more introspective." Llewellyn Davies.

unfrequently led to results the very reverse of useful.

There is need, no doubt, to examine into your moral condition, in order that the comparison of what you are with what you should be may shame you into fresh efforts at reformation and progress: but, except so far as it leads to this result, self-examination has absolutely no moral worth. On the contrary it tends directly and powerfully to retard all true progress by fixing men's attention on what is past instead of in the work which lies before them in the future. The time that is taken up in bemoaning past transgressions would always be better employed in repairing them. "Nature the sovereign physician bids us let our wounds alone, live healthily, do right and leave the rest to her[1]."

It is not *inwards* but *forwards* and *upwards*

---

[1] Froude, cf. also Rev. F. W. Robertson, "He who can dwell on this or that symptom of his moral nature is already diseased. Redemption is to *forget* self in God." Cf. also Wordsworth, "That man whose eye is ever on himself, Doth look on one, the least of nature's works."

that we should look, if we would do our fair share of the work which it is given us to do. In proof of this being the true view we may quote the example of St Paul, who describes himself as "Forgetting those things which are behind and reaching forth unto those things which are before[1]."

Enough has now been said to shew that *introspection* cannot hold in an ethical point of view the important place which the advocates of Confession are agreed in assigning to it. Again, it is not only by absorbing energies that might otherwise have been given to the work of moral progress, that excessive self-examination is productive of harm. It has another result which requires to be noticed, and which is even more to be dreaded.

It is a well-established principle of mental science that *ideas* have a tendency to become actualities[2]. An idea of an action is in fact only the action itself in a weaker form. "Temptation

---

[1] Phil. iii. 13, 14.

[2] Cf. Bain's *Mental Science*.

Also Kant, *Metaph. of Ethics*, "All determination of choice whatever begins with the representation of the intended act."

to do something forbidden often comes of merely suggesting the idea, which is then a power to act itself out[1]."

Now it is easy to see how this applies to the matter before us. The constant search after, and minute enquiry into faults, which are so strictly enjoined by Confessors, and in aid of which an elaborate code of questions has been drawn up, cannot fail to be a frequent source of moral danger.

We have, indeed, too high an opinion of the character of the English Clergy, to think it likely that this power of putting questions would be often abused in the particular way in which some zealous opponents of the Confessional have chosen to suppose; and that questions prescribed for extreme and exceptional cases would be made use of to shock and insult pureminded persons[2]. There is

---

[1] Bain, p. 90.

[2] There is no denying the abuses to which this power of questioning has given rise in Roman Catholic countries and its corrupting influence on the priests themselves.

Cf. *Confessions of a French Catholic priest*, edited by S. F. B. Morse, M.A., Rev. W. Hogan's *Auricular Confession and Popish Nunneries*, and Mrs E. Richardson's *Personal experiences of Roman Catholicism*, &c.

nevertheless serious reason to dread the results of this perpetual examination and questioning, which, however conscientiously employed, cannot fail to familiarise the mind with sin, and thereby lessen in some degree the horror with which it is at first regarded. That there is real danger of this can be shewn by the admission of many who have yet been supporters of the Confessional on the ground of its divine origin.

Marcus Eremita, who lived when the auricular Confession was in its infancy, says—"If thou wilt offer to God an irreproachable Confession, do not recount thy sins *particularly, for so thou dost defile thy mind;* but generously endure their assaults or what they have brought upon thee."

Again it was proposed by Cardinal Cajetan as a "case of conscience," Utrum confessor cognoscens ex his quæ audit in confessione, sequi in seipso emissionem seminis sibi displicentem, peccet mor-

---

An English Clergyman, however, from the circumstances of his position and early training may be supposed to be free from many of the special temptations which have proved so fatal to Continental priests.

B. E.

taliter audiendo vel persequendo tales confessiones?" Another Cardinal gives the following as his solution of the difficulty—"Confessarius, si forte dum audit confessiones in tales incidit pollutiones, non ob id tenetur non audire alios, nisi sit periculum complacentiæ in pollutione, tunc enim tenetur relinquere confessiones, et auferre peccati occasionem, secus non[1]."

The existence of a Bull of Pius IV. "Contra Sollicitantes in Confessione"[2] is a further proof that the enquiry into and examination of sins was an admitted source of moral danger, even in comparatively early times. This danger, indeed, to which priest and penitent are alike exposed, has been so frequently pointed out that there can be no need to pile up a mass of evidence in support of it[3]. We will therefore conclude with the description of it

[1] Lib. 5, *Inst. Sacerd.* c. 3, sub. fig. 5.
[2] Bull of Pius IV. to Bp of Seville, 1561. (*Narrative of the Inquisition*, by H. J. Da Costa, Vol. I. p. 119.)
There was a similar Bull of Greg. XV. in 1622.
[3] The article on Confession framed by the German Reformers and adopted and corrected by Archbp Cranmer, makes a full admission of the danger in question in its 6th clause.
Further information on the subject will be found in Michelet's *Priests, Women and Families*, where the dangers to which priests in particular are exposed are forcibly illustrated.

which has been given by the author of the *Imitation of Christ*. After citing with approval the advice of Ovid to withstand the beginnings of evil, Thomas à Kempis goes on to say, "For first there cometh to the mind a bare *thought* (of evil), then a strong *imagination* thereof, afterwards *delight* and an evil motion and then *consent;* and so by little and little our wicked enemy getteth complete entrance." The process which he thus describes is one with which every student of mental philosophy must be familiar, and it would be well if our religious teachers were equally sensible of the bad effects of that continual dwelling on the worst side of a man's nature which the Confessional does so much to encourage.

Again, not only has Confession a dangerous tendency to infuse bad qualities, but it is directly destructive of many that from an ethical point of view are of the highest value.

See also, *The Priest, the Woman and the Confessional* by Père Chiniquy, p. 3; *The Confessional and its consequences* by A Wife and a Mother; *Confessions of a Roman Catholic Priest*, Edited by S. F. B. Morse, M.A.; *Personal Experiences of Roman Catholicism* by Eliza Richardson, &c.

Self-respect, for example, though liable like other qualities to be unduly exaggerated, is an important *aid* to virtue[1], and it can hardly be expected to live long under the influence of the Confessional. The sense of Shame, too, which Carlyle has called the "Soil of all virtue, of all good manners and good morals," will naturally interfere with the Confessor's work of examination, and so far as it has a tendency to do this, he will feel it a duty to root it out[2].

If he should succeed in doing this, as is only too probable, one of the strongest props of virtue will be taken away and the chances of falling consequently greatly increased.

There is another grave objection against Confession which is nearly connected with some of

---

[1] The manner in which qualities and motives, which have no *absolute* worth of their own, can assist in the work of moral progress, was pointed out in an earlier part of this Essay when the general principles of progress were being discussed.

[2] "*Pudor ille vicendus*, Sacrilega foret confessio quæ *tam vano motivo* decutaretur," Pœnitentia (by Delahogue), p. 164. Remorse for past sin is another "aid to virtue" which will naturally be destroyed by a system which teaches that absolution restores a sinner to the favour of God by its own inherent virtue.

those we have just been considering and which we cannot afford to pass over.

The advocates of Confession have often shewn themselves contemptuously ignorant of the laws and conditions of moral progress, and never more so than in their neglect of the part which trust and confidence in a man's power to raise himself can play in aiding him to do so.

Experience has repeatedly proved that the way to get a man to do his duty is, not to be perpetually suspecting him and questioning him as to his motives, but to shew that you have faith in his good intentions and in his ability to carry them out. Suspicion has invariably a blighting and hardening influence, while there is no more powerful agent in the work of moral reform than a large and generous faith, which lays hold of what is good in a man's nature and seeks to draw it out, no matter what sins and weaknesses may lie concealed beneath it. These may be trusted to die out in proportion as the other sides of his character gain in strength; for, good and evil being by nature opposed, growth of the one necessarily implies decay of the other.

And here we are brought to the threshold of a great truth, which lies at the bottom of all this part of our subject, and forms the ground of some of the gravest of the objections urged against Confession. Human nature is so constituted that you cannot get rid of one quality except by substituting another for it. Just as matter and force cannot be annihilated in the world of nature, and death in one form is always followed by new life in another, so in the moral world there is no such thing as simple and absolute destruction. In other words, there is no such thing as a state of *sinlessness* as opposed to a state of *positive goodness*. You cannot cease to be *bad* except by becoming *good*. It is to the expulsive power of good desires and to this alone, that you must look for the eradication of bad desires. A great painter has given it as his opinion that "*affirmative* teaching alone is of any avail in art:" that "criticism and demonstration of defects give little help and no inspiration," and that "only familiarity with what is excellent preserves from what is false[1]"; and this observation is no less true when applied to morals than when applied to art[2]. It will avail nothing to point out and scrutinize defects, unless you are prepared with something to put in their place. You may convince by your arguments, but you will produce no effect in getting rid of the obnoxious qualities.

No one who has had to face the problem of how to eradicate a bad habit, will question the truth of these remarks, and their bearing on the principles and teaching of the Confessionalists must be obvious enough. The system of questioning and examination, in which the value of Confession is mainly thought to consist, is defensible only on the assumption that *sinlessness* (not

---

[1] Hippolyte Flandrin.
[2] Cf. also Wm. von Humboldt. "We develop the Artist by accustoming his eye to dwell on the great masterpieces of artistic skill; we expand his imagination by a study of the faultlessly beautiful models of antiquity; and in like manner must the process of moral development be effected through the contemplation of loftier moral perfection."

positive goodness) is the end to be aimed at, and that bad qualities can be got rid of directly without the necessity of cultivating their opposites. This position is tenable enough for those who believe in a divine proffer of forgiveness through the medium of Confession and priestly Absolution; but it is difficult to see how those who profess to defend Confession on ethical principles can make this assumption fit in with any theory of moral progress.

Passing now from the harm that is done by the excessive importance which Confession attributes to introspection and examination of faults, we have to consider another way in which it is likely to have a bad effect on the character of those who resort to it.

There is a mistaken view of the nature of repentance and its consequences which the Confessional is extremely apt to encourage, and which exercises a most pernicious influence whenever it is found to prevail. Confession, if made in a spirit of contrition and followed by absolution, is thought to place the repentant sinner in the same position as though he had never fallen[1].

The Abbé Gaume indeed goes further, and maintains that "Confession and repentance have more power to raise men than sin has to cast them down[2]"; but the less extravagant view is probably the commoner among the modern adherents of Confession.

Now here again it is worth while pointing out that there is nothing to be surprised at in this opinion being held by the advocates of what we have called the "Sacramental" view of Confession. If Confession is a divinely instituted means of obtaining forgiveness, endowed with a special and superhuman efficacy, there can be nothing unreasonable in supposing it to have a miraculous power of effacing all the consequences of sin. When once

---

[1] Keble remarks, "The tradition that goes by the name of 'Justification by Faith' in reality means that one who has sinned and is sorry for it, is as if he had not sinned," and he speaks of its "blighting and benumbing" influence.

Again, in the Article on Confession in *Books for the Young*, it is said, "When you have received it (absolution) you are pure and spotless as on the day when you were baptised."

[2] *Manual for Confessors* (Pusey's Translation).

a miracle is allowed to be in question, we cannot pronounce anything to be impossible. But those who profess to believe in the human origin of Confession, and deny that it has any results which cannot be accounted for on purely human principles, cannot without the grossest inconsistency believe in the effects thus ascribed to it.

Let us take the case of a man who makes Confession of an habitual sin, and on shewing true contrition receives absolution from his Confessor. It surely cannot be maintained by anyone who disbelieves in the miraculous element in Confession and Absolution that the habit has ceased to be a part of the sinner's nature, and that he is henceforth free from any special liability to fall into that particular sin! Clearly a miracle is wanted to accomplish a change like this. On human principles habits cannot be so lightly and easily shaken off. They may be gradually supplanted by the cultivation of other and opposite habits, but their removal must always be a work of time and difficulty, and there is no weapon in man's moral armoury by which they can be suddenly destroyed. There is really nothing irreverent in this view, as some perhaps may be inclined to object.

The wisdom and goodness of God are shewn as much in his general laws as in his special interferences with them, and of these laws there is none better established than that which regulates the growth and decay of *habits*. Man's duty is to make himself acquainted with these laws and to guide his steps in conformity with them, and he has no right to murmur because the task is not always an easy one and his progress is often gradual and slow. We are always too ready to believe that there must be a shorter and easier way to perfection than the rugged, toilsome path of duty, and it is one of the gravest of the many charges that can be brought against Confession that it directly and powerfully encourages this tendency.

The true meaning and value of repentance for past sin is, *not* that it restores the sinner to his former state, and wipes away his sin and its consequences; but that it turns his face again to the path of duty from which he has gone astray, and brings him once more into harmony with the work of moral progress. He has to recommence this work at a lower level than that to which he had before attained, and with powers weakened by his fall;—such is the unavoidable result of sin—but, to be once more labouring for the right; to be building up instead of destroying; aiding instead of retarding the work which divine wisdom has appointed—surely this is enough to give importance and value to repentance, without supposing it to be endowed with any miraculous efficacy such as the adherents of Confession have been accustomed to claim for it.

This feeling of coming once more into harmony with God's purposes; of sympathising with his plans, and being admitted again into the ranks of his servants; is what constitutes the essence of that peace which penitence is so often found to give.

If it is any other peace than this that is

sought:—whether it be the peace of a stifled or neglected conscience; or the peace that comes from making over your cares to another's keeping and resolving to act and think henceforth as he shall direct: whichever of these it may be, such peace is worthless and bad, and so far as the Confessional is resorted to as a means of producing it, it is the cause of infinite mischief.

There is no more fatal error to which men are liable than that of mistaking the quiet of a neglected conscience for the peace of an approving one, and fancying that all must be well because the voice of self-accusation is no longer heard within. It is the longing for peace after inward strife and discord that drives men to the Confessional; but the calm which it undoubtedly gives is too often the calm which tells of decaying faculties and approaching spiritual death, and not the quiet unimpeded flow of life and health[1].

We have now examined at sufficient length the

[1] Cf. Whately, "In all ages and countries man is more desirous of a quiet than of a vigilant and tender conscience; studious to escape the thought of spiritual danger, more than the danger itself."

most important of the ways in which Confession will be likely to have an injurious influence on men's moral characters; and we have seen that many of its results are such as may naturally be expected whenever Confession is regarded as an *end in itself*, or as a means only to absolution;— from which point of view, indeed, they are reasonable and unobjectionable enough.

If divine forgiveness waits on Confession and Absolution; introspection and self-examination, being essential to this, must be inculcated as much as possible, and nothing that has been urged against their moral tendency can be allowed to have any weight.

So, too, all that has been said of the need of cultivating good habits as the sole means of eradicating bad ones, falls to the ground at once, since in *absolution* we have an easier and more expeditious way of effecting their expulsion.

Again, the theory of repentance and its consequences, which we have been criticising on ethical grounds, becomes plausible and credible at once when regarded from the point of view of the "Sacramentalists;" and true spiritual peace can be had on easier terms than those just laid down, and need no longer imply a return to moral activity.

To those however who have conceded that Confession is only a human institution, acting in accordance with the laws and principles of human nature and having nothing supernatural about it, there is no such way of evading the charges brought against Confession, and the facts and arguments we have been engaged in reviewing remain to be faced in their full and unabated force.

It is doubtful, indeed, whether a consistent attempt ever has been or ever will be made to defend Confession on purely ethical grounds. When arguments have been drawn from the moral aspect of the question they have commonly been employed as a sort of external defence or "outworks," while the main reliance has ever been placed on the "power of the Keys[1]," that mys-

[1] See Appendix on *Sacramental Theory*.

terious tower of Strength, which affords a sure retreat when other defences fail, and which the arguments of moralists will always assault in vain! Even when the "sacramental" theory (as it is termed) is not expressly avowed, it will be found on investigation to be at the bottom of most of the reasoning employed on behalf of Confession, and it has been shewn in the preceding pages that many of the qualities and practices which it is the special aim of the Confessional to produce, are defensible only on the assumption that this theory is the true one.

It is time now to pass to the *fourth* and last division of our subject, and give our attention to the *social* aspect of Confession ; or, in other words, to the *indirect* effect which it is likely to have upon moral character through its influence on the different relations in which men stand to one another as members of one common Society.

Its *direct* effect as a moral agent is what we have hitherto been considering, but this is not enough, as has been already pointed out, to enable us to give a satisfactory judgment on the whole question.

Confession cannot do its work without influencing other institutions, each of which has a certain power of aiding moral progress; and the degree in which this power is increased or retarded by it will naturally be an important factor in determining the general result.

So much has been said in an early part of this Essay of the general conditions which all institutions must fulfil in order to be of use, that there can be no need here for anything further on that head, and we may therefore pass at once to the most important of those institutions on which social life is based, and proceed to note the effect which Confession is likely to produce upon them.

It is natural to begin with "*The Family*," since it is as a disturber of the relations of family life that the practice of Confession has been most frequently and fiercely opposed.

The assailants of Confession have occasionally let their zeal carry them a little too far, and have not unfrequently brought forward charges which they have been unable to substantiate; but there is no reason to think them guilty of injustice in their unsparing abuse of its domestic tendencies. Facts and Statistics fully bear them out in what they have said on this point[1].

The Confessional is directly opposed to all that is most valuable in family life, and no means exist

---

[1] It has been claimed for the Confessional that it is found to be a powerful deterrent from Crime, and especially from such crimes as are offences against family life. Cf. A layman's view of Confession, *Studies in Modern Problems*, Part 2.

This however has been clearly disproved by the Statistics collected by Mr Hobart Seymour (*The Confessional*). In the Tables of comparative morality which he has compiled the advantage is unmistakably with the countries where the Confessional is not in common use.

In an interesting letter recounting his experience in France and Spain, a Doctor, who enjoyed unusually favourable opportunities of forming a judgment on the matter, describes the domestic morality of those countries as so thoroughly undermined, "that only a sweeping change in religion can save either of them from utter decay." *Echo*, Aug. 1, 1877.

We have abstained from entering on the historical aspect of the subject as not coming within the legitimate scope of this Essay, but it is impossible to doubt that the deplorable domestic condition of Southern Europe as depicted by Hallam and Lecky must be set down partly to the corrupting influence of the Confessional and the temptations with which it is attended.

by which the two institutions can be brought to work in harmony.

The most rational and consistent view for an advocate of Confession to take would be that, in virtue of its superior sanctity (as being of divine origin), Confession has a right to prevail over family influence in cases where the two conflict; but it is useless to deny the existence of any conflict as some have attempted to do.

For what is it that gives its special value to life in a family and makes it so important in a moral point of view? Is it not its freedom from all restraint but that which natural affections and sense of filial duty afford, and the opportunity which it therefore gives for the growth and development of those qualities which forms and systems of government have always a tendency to blight and wither? And is not this freedom which exists in the family as it exists nowhere else, the very thing which Confession does most to destroy?

The true moral significance of family life has

been so commonly mistaken that it may be worth our while to dwell a little upon it.

Progress, in morals, as in politics, invariably takes the form and direction of increasing liberty, and to judge fairly of the value of family life, we must be careful to view it in connection with this fact. Man was not meant to be kept for ever in forced obedience to his fellow men, and every fresh step of moral advance he takes implies a proportionate relaxation of his bonds. Pure affections take the place of ignoble fear, and the harsh rigour of outward law is succeeded by the gentler rule of love. Such is the path of progress, which, starting from brute impulse, leads men on from one desire to another, till it ends in the sole dominion of that love of right and duty which is only another aspect of the will of God.

It is in keeping before men's eyes the image of a higher and purer state than that which the outer world with its systems of laws and government affords, and in directly fostering those qualities which, as they grow in strength, render the need for such outward discipline ever less and less; that family life fulfils its highest mission and shews itself in its divinest aspect. Surely, then, that system must be condemned which aims at introducing artificial restraints and regulations into the very heart of the family[1], checking the free play of natural affections, and destroying the kindly flow of sympathy by trying to divert it into a new and unnatural channel.

For, what sympathy can there be between priest and penitent like that which subsists between husband and wife, between parent and child? and where there is no real sympathy there can be no real power for good in any form of human intercourse.

It is not meant, of course, that natural affection will be wholly destroyed by the intrusion of a

---

[1] "In families it introduces untold mischief. It supersedes God's appointment of intimacy between Husband and Wife, Father and Children; substituting another influence for that which ought to be the nearest and closest, and producing reserve and estrangement where there ought to be perfect *freedom* and openness." Bp Wilberforce (at a conference at Winchester House). *Record*, May 15, 1874.

priest into the affairs of a family. It has its roots too far down in human nature to be pulled up easily and at once. But, though family feeling may be expected to survive, it will be robbed of its choicest fruits.

There is nothing of inherent moral value in the mere natural affections which man possesses in common with the beasts.

It is only so far as they aid in his moral development and give life and vigour to the work of mutual help, that these affections rise to moral worth; and it is precisely their power of doing this that the Confessional aims to deprive them of.

The part which they were intended to play in aid of moral culture is taken from them and made over to a priest, and they consequently sink back at once to the level of mere animal affections[1].

The advocates of Confession seem to think that

[1] In *What is Coming* or *The Confessional in England*, a case is mentioned where an Anglican "Confessor" told a lady that "she had no right to tell anybody she had been to Confession." On her saying, "I thought we ought to tell our husbands everything," he replied, "True, they should not be deceived; but Confession is a thing you ought not to tell them, *it concerns your souls and not your bodies!*"

they have given a sufficient answer to those who condemn its influence on family life, if they have succeeded in shewing that parents continue to love their children, and affectionate husbands and wives are to be found in countries where the Confessional is in common use. All this may very readily be conceded, as it does not at all affect our position that Confession tends to impair the *moral* value of family life.

A parent's love for his children is a thing of little worth, if it leads to no effort for their moral welfare. If there is to be silence between them on all that concerns the deeper wants of their nature; if faults and failings, temptations and spiritual trials, are to be kept hidden from each other and revealed only to the secret eye of the priest[1]; if there is to be no sympathetic communing of soul with soul; no bearing of one another's burdens; what will it avail in such a case that parents and children, husband and wife, continue to dwell

---

[1] "It is to the priest, and to *the priest only*, that a child must acknowledge his sins, if he desires that God should forgive him." *Books for the Young*, No. 1, "Confession."

together and to feel for each other an affection out of which all the deeper moral meaning has passed away?

This tendency of the Confessional to destroy the moral influence of family life is of far more importance than any of the particular and incidental evils by which it is attended, and on which so much stress has commonly been laid. There can be no need to repeat here what has been said of the danger of divulging family secrets to a priest: of the mischievous results of a divided rule and the petty tyranny sometimes exercised by priests over families: of the increased danger of family divisions, and of estrangement between husband and wife[1].

[1] Facts and statistics on these points which are too numerous to quote will be found in Rev. M. H. Seymour's *Moral results of the Romish system*, and M. Michelet's *Priests, Women and Families*. A very few illustrations may be given from other sources.

Dr Jelf (*Examination into Doctrine and Practice of Confession*) says, "I have heard of a case in which to a girl's plea that to do what the priest ordered her would involve disobedience to her parents' wishes, it was answered that this would make it all the more meritorious, according to a well-known passage, 'He that loveth father and mother,' &c."

Mr Hobart Seymour says, "This is the great practical evil of the Confessional. It places the secret of every woman, if her confession be full, in the hands of the Priest, and she is thus *in his power*. It

These evils are for the most part such as will naturally suggest themselves, and they are all subordinate to the main objection which has just been urged.

The subject of Confession has been viewed by the majority of those who have treated of it in altogether too narrow a light. Undue importance has been given to matters of detail and incidental results, while the general character and tendency of the institution have been comparatively neglected.

It has been the aim of this Essay to treat the subject in a broader and more philosophical spirit, and to bring it to the test of more fundamental

places the secret of every man, if indeed he confesses fully, in the hands of the Priest, and he is from that moment *his slave*. It places both priest and penitent in a wrong and false position. It places them both in a position too trying for flesh and blood. The penitent is liable also to reveal all his knowledge of the *sins of others*. The power which this system gives is a terrible engine." (*The Confessional.*)

Again the Rev. W. Anderson says, "The man who has revealed the secrets of his heart to a Confessor, has surrendered his liberty, and with his liberty the highest moral, intellectual and spiritual capacities of his nature. People trained under such a discipline as this will carry all through their life the marks of their bondage." *A Lecture delivered before the Exeter Branch of the Church Association.*

principles than those by which it has commonly been tried.

Passing now to another head of our subject, we shall see that Confession is no less opposed to the spirit of *Political* life in all its forms than it has been shewn to be to that of *Family* life.

Indeed the opposition here is if possible more marked and is of the deepest possible kind, as a very short explanation will suffice to shew.

All forms and systems of Government, however otherwise opposed they may be, are alike in this, that they are based on one universal principle (of which they are but different applications); and to this principle Confession has at all times shewn itself unceasingly hostile.

Co-operation or "Division of Labour," as (more especially in its industrial aspect) it has been styled, is the principle which is at the bottom of and gives value to all the varied forms which political life assumes throughout the world.

It is found that by combining and uniting their efforts men can do more for their common good than by isolating themselves and working each for himself. Nor is it *material* good alone that is promoted by division of labour. Its *moral* consequences, though less frequently recognised, are of even greater importance[1], and it needs only to glance at the way in which sciences have been built up by the labours of successive generations:— the facts collected in one age being used in support of theories put forward in another, to convince us of its vast influence also in the *intellectual* world.

It is man's lot to be placed in a finite world where he is subject to the conditions of Time and Space, but, by a skilful application of the principle of division of labour, he is able to free himself from many of the restraints which they would otherwise impose upon him.

For instance, though he cannot be working in two places at one and the same time, yet, acting on the principle we are considering, he can exchange the products of his labour with the dweller in

---

[1] "Genus humanum maxime Deo assimilatur, quando maxime est *unum*, quando *totum unitur in uno.*" (Dante, *Monarchia* i.)

another hemisphere, and so get some of the advantages which an omnipresent being might be supposed to enjoy in full.

Again, he cannot in the short space of a lifetime work his unassisted way to the heights of science, but the path has been prepared for him, and tools made ready for his hands by the labour of those who have gone before him. Thus the co-operation of the Past with the Present destroys the worst effects of *Time*.

To return again to the *political* aspect of division of labour. Experience has shewn that the work of progress will proceed more rapidly if one part of it is assigned to one man (or set of men) and another part to another, than if each were left to attempt the whole task for himself.

To one set of men therefore is allotted the special task of giving spiritual aid and guidance. Again the physical power of the community is put under the direction of another set, that it may be employed in the shape of *punishments*, and so bring to the aid of duty the deterring power of *fear*.

This same power, again, is entrusted to another set of persons for a different purpose, viz. to guard the community from any external dangers that may threaten it. And similarly, throughout all the most important *aids to progress*, which experience has pointed out, we see a special part and power assigned to those who have given proof of special fitness. In rude and early stages of social life, all or many of these functions are frequently united in one person. The co-operation in such cases is of the most rudimentary kind, the division being simply that into governor and governed, leader and followers. Even this state of things, however, is better than the anarchy which preceded it, and each successive advance that is made implies increased co-operation and division of labour.

Those who have a special power of benefiting the community in one direction begin to devote themselves principally to its cultivation, having their other wants supplied by those whom special training or opportunities have fitted for the task.

Thus we see that co-operation and interaction are the great law of political life. Isolation of interests and regard for *self* are directly opposed to its whole spirit and are absolutely incompatible with any of its higher forms.

Yet these are the very qualities which Confession has always made it its special aim to produce and cultivate. Those who seek its help are told to keep their attention fixed on their inward state, and allow no thought of worldly things to make them neglect the sacred task of saving their own souls from perdition[1].

Political and Social interests, they are taught, are things of little worth when compared with the inner life of the soul. So long as this latter is attended to and kept free from deadly sins, it

---

[1] "Doubtless your first duty is to work out your own sanctification." Abbé Gaume.

This is to be done by the aid of *penances* in the consideration of which a great part of the Abbé's book is taken up. Among penances are mentioned *Prayers* and *Sacraments* and even *Communions*—four "Our Fathers" being accounted an "easy penance," p. 356.

The great majority of those mentioned by Gaume have received Dr Pusey's sanction, one or two only of the most extravagant ones being declared unsuited for Anglican use. [*Manual for Confessors.*]

matters little what amount of interest is taken in the practical affairs of the world.

As these are frequently found to have a disturbing influence, in drawing a man out of himself and making him forget his own salvation in his concern for common interests, it is thought to be the safer plan to have as little to do with them as possible.

If, however, a man is not able or willing to keep aloof from them altogether, he must still be careful to keep their worldly nature ever before his eyes, and never let himself be deceived into thinking that a life spent in framing laws or discharging public duties can have as much merit in the eyes of God as a life of religious fervour and inward humility.

Politics and social institutions, it is said, relate to man's temporal wants, as a dweller in a finite world; whereas religion has to do with the divine element in his nature, and is charged with the care of his immortal soul.

If, then, you give more thought to the practical affairs of life than to the state of your own soul, you are exalting what is *finite* over what is *infinite*, what is *human* above what is *divine;* and how, if this be so, can you avoid the charge of impiety?

Such is the view commonly taken by the advocates of Confession of the relations of religion and politics, and such the kind of reasoning by which it is commonly supported.

That neither the one nor the other has been exaggerated will be readily admitted by all who are acquainted with Manuals of Confession, and their influence, if they should ever prevail, on the whole spirit of political life may easily be imagined. We are far too apt, as it is, to overlook the *moral* side of politics and to keep our attention fixed on its lower aspects. Things are not unfrequently done by political bodies, which the men who compose them would be ashamed to do as private individuals; the notion seeming to be that conscience, as an *individual* thing, can have no jurisdiction over joint-action of any kind!

If, then, under existing circumstances there is a dangerous prevalence of low and sordid views of politics, how much greater will this danger become if the Confessional and the doctrines associated with it are allowed to re-assert themselves! It is impossible to imagine a more pernicious theory, or one more likely to corrupt and deprave political life, than that which teaches the utter worthlessness, as compared with religion, of forms and systems of government and institutions of every kind. How can we expect politics to be anything but a "selfish struggle" for place and power, if all its higher significance is to be taken from it, as it would be if the Confessionalists had their way?

For the fact that the men who are seeking to revive the Confessional are those who have been most strenuous in insisting on the absolute difference in scope and aim between religion and politics, is no mere coincidence, as some may perhaps be inclined to suppose.

Whenever and wherever the Confessional has become an established practice, this theory has been found to prevail, and it is not difficult to find reasons why this should be so.

The common way of accounting for the hostility which "priests" have so uniformly shewn to political life, and for their refusal to allow real worth to any institutions but their own, has been to set it all down to unscrupulous ambition and a wish to subject everything to themselves.

Now ambition and love of power have no doubt played an important part in the history of the Church, and it would be absurd to suppose that they have no influence at the present day; but we should, in our opinion, be guilty of great unfairness to a conscientious and well meaning set of men, if we were to take these to be the motives that are actuating the bulk of the modern advocates of Confession.

If, then, we cannot explain the connection between their advocacy of Confession and their attitude towards political life by simply regarding them as two different forms of priestly arrogance and ambition; in what direction are we to look for a more just and reasonable explanation?

It is to be found, we think, in the prevalence of

two theories, one or other of which is almost invariably held by the class of men we are alluding to.

The *first* is that which has frequently been called attention to in the course of this Essay, under the name of the "Sacramental" theory of Confession. Confession is regarded by the great body of its defenders as a special medium of divine favour and grace, which only requires to be supplemented by priestly absolution in order to wipe off the effects of past sin.

This miraculous efficacy is sometimes made dependent on the condition of the penitent, but it is always maintained that something more takes place than can be accounted for on simple ethical principles.

Now it is natural enough that those who take this view of Confession should think lightly of the importance of political institutions. However useful they may be thought to be, it was never claimed for them that they had any superhuman power of effacing sin and realising a divine promise of forgiveness, and they are therefore on an entirely different footing from Confession, and cannot even be compared to it without something approaching to impiety. The attitude which the Tractarians took up with regard to the connection of Church and State was a natural consequence of that belief in "Apostolical Succession" and the "Power of the Keys" which was at the bottom of their zeal for Confession.

In short, so far as we find men adhering to the "Sacramental" view of Confession, so far must we expect to find politics degraded to the level of a mere worldly occupation and robbed of all that gives it its highest value in the eyes of the moralist.

The *second* of the two theories by which the defenders of Confession seem to be influenced in their opposition to political life, is one which deserves to be attentively considered, as it possesses a sufficient basis of truth to make it exceedingly dangerous.

It is maintained, in opposition to all forms of Utilitarianism, that moral worth belongs to the inward character of a man,—his desires, thoughts and affections—and has nothing to do with his outward *acts* and their consequences.

Among the different forms of political and social life, there are some which are allowed to be more fitting and proper than others; but the merit which belongs to them is altogether of a different kind from that which is claimed for the affections and desires, and is not to be compared with it in importance. Hence it follows that the sole concern of Confessors and religious teachers of all kinds should be for the inward state of those who seek their aid, and, in devoting themselves to this, they will be taking up a position to which no ruler or guide of outward action can ever hope to aspire.

This, or something like this, appears to be the view of a large number of the supporters of the Confessional, and it contains (in our opinion), together with much that is pernicious, an important element of truth.

We do not hold, any more than those whose views we are about to criticise, that absolute moral worth can be attributed to any kind of *acts*, and quite agree that it properly belongs only to the inner forces which make up a man's character.

Indeed, we have gone further than this (it will be remembered), and allowed *absolute* value to one motive only by which men are actuated, viz., the love of right or duty; and considered all others to be good only in the degree in which they aid in the development and strengthening of this motive.

In other words, their importance and value is that which belongs to *means*, not *ends;* and this *relative* value is all that in our opinion can rightly be ascribed to *acts*.

An act implies that one motive has resisted and overcome another or others, and is to be pronounced good so far, and so far only, as this conquest facilitates the development of the love of duty[1].

But though *absolute* moral value is thus denied

---

[1] The theory of progress here alluded to, is set forth in the early part of this Essay.

to acts, it is not meant that they may on that account be neglected or treated as unimportant; and it is here that the difference between our view and the one we are finding fault with comes out most clearly. Though acts are means, they are *necessary* means, and no moral progress can be made without them. Moral and Spiritual perfection can never be attained by directly aiming at it, as those imagine who affect to despise the *practical* side of life. The world of outward action is the field where the inward forces gather strength and nourishment, and, whenever their proper exercise is denied them, they are invariably found to dwindle and decay.

It is therefore a fatal error into which those have fallen who make light of the practical work of the world, and insist only on the possession of a right inward state. Yet it is one which extensively prevails, and nowhere more so than among the adherents of Confession[1].

[1] The contempt which they entertain for "practical" life is well illustrated by their system of penances.

Instead of enjoining active employment and encouraging penitents

It is an error very similar in its nature to that of some modern enthusiasts for liberty, who seeing that non-interference with others' rights must be one of the characteristics of a perfected humanity, assume that *non-interference* is the right rule to follow at the present day; or that, if any allowance has to be made for present weakness and imperfection, an equal apportionment of the unavoidable restraint will be enough to meet the difficulty[1].

A little reflection ought to shew, however, that if men should ever reach this ideal state where non-interference (or *negative* assistance) is all that is needed, and where each man is sufficient to himself,—it will only be because innumerable ages of

to take part in works of common interest as a means of shaking off their sin and its consequences, they are in the habit of prescribing a certain number of prayers or attendances at Communion, or they suggest such remedies as the following:—As a remedy against Impurity, (1) To fortify the forehead or breast with the sign of the Cross; (2) To bring before the penitent's imagination a corpse in a state of corruption! &c. [*The Priest in Absolution.*]

[1] Herbert Spencer's *Law of Equal Freedom* is particularly alluded to here (Social Statics), but the criticism has a general application to all theories of Government which profess to rest on a system of *absolute* rights.

positive assistance and mutual help have preceded it and made it possible.

Short cuts to perfection have always proved delusive, and yet such theories have seldom any difficulty in finding supporters.

Men's beliefs are so much the result of their desires that they have always a favourable ear for any one who will tell them of an easy way out of their difficulties, whether these difficulties be political, moral, or religious.

Enough has now been said respecting the mistake of those who think that because true goodness consists in the possession of a right inward state, they must therefore make this the direct and immediate object of pursuit and can afford to neglect the more practical affairs of life. Wherever this theory prevails, rites and ceremonies, fasts and penances: everything, in short, that is directly efficacious in stirring up religious feelings, will be found to grow in number and importance; and the growth of these will invariably be followed by the decline of political life and of all the varied forms of combined action on which the progress of the world depends.

This theory, as was before remarked, is one which seems to be very generally accepted by the modern advocates of Confession; and its influence, taken together with that of the "Sacramental" theory, is amply sufficient to account for the position which they have commonly taken up with regard to the relation of politics and religion.

It is not necessary to repeat what has before been said of the evil results of the degradation of political life which must inevitably follow. It is important to note, however, that they are of far wider scope and deeper import than has commonly been supposed. Attention has frequently been directed to particular evils; such as the danger of entrusting State secrets to Confessors; and the opportunity which will be given to them of exalting the ecclesiastical at the expense of the civil power. History has been appealed to in proof of the mischievous results of priestly influence,— the probable decline of science and learning, the growth of intolerance and bigotry, and the diffusion of superstitious and unmanly follies. But, while all these things have been loudly insisted on, the far wider objection, which it has been attempted to bring out in these pages, has never, so far as we are aware, been touched upon. Certainly it has never received the attention it can justly claim.

It is not for this or that particular evil that Confession is to be condemned in a political point of view: but because it is opposed, directly and entirely, to the whole spirit of political life; and not of political life only, but of every form of social intercourse by which men are bound together and their power for good increased.

Every social institution owes whatever moral excellence may belong to it to the superiority of *combined* over *individual* action; and to the degree in which it enables men to rise above their own selfish interests to larger sympathies and views. Confession, on the other hand, tends to keep a man absorbed and engrossed in the contemplation of his own inner state. It tells him that the salvation of his own soul should be each man's chief concern, and undertakes to shew him how this salvation can be obtained at the least expense of labour and suffering! The object of a man's life according to this view, is, not to do the greatest possible amount of good, but to avoid as many deadly sins as possible, and to get the fullest absolution for such of them as he cannot help committing. His duty, in short, is *negative* not *positive*, consisting of *forbearances* instead of *acts;* the only acts to which any value at all is conceded being such as experience shews to have a direct effect in stimulating the religious feelings[1].

Now this seems to us to be a low and degrading view of human life and its purposes, whether we regard it as a moral theory, or as an article of religious faith.

As a moral theory, it can only claim to rank among the lower forms of "Egoism," and must be put infinitely below the more refined Utili-

[1] Bp Wilberforce describes Confession as "a system of unnatural excitement, a sort of spiritual dram-drinking fraught with evil to the whole spiritual constitution."

tarianism which prevails at the present day,—to say nothing of its inferiority to other and professedly higher ethical schemes.

In a *religious* point of view, again, it is an insult to the Deity to suppose that he sent men into the world for no better purpose than to save themselves; each for himself, from an impending damnation.

If there is any force in the analogy of nature, if there is any truth in the Christian Revelation, mankind have a real *positive* work to accomplish in this life, and can never have been intended to make a mere negative immunity from punishment the final aim and object of their existence. This work, too, is one which can never be done by solitary individual action of any kind, but requires for its due fulfilment the combined efforts of all who love the right. The world of nature shews us no force which works apart in solitary seclusion, uninfluencing and uninfluenced by the other forces of the Universe. Each of these has a part to perform in the furtherance of one common work, and assists, according to its measure, in the fulfilment of one universal purpose.

The Christian Revelation, again, has taught us, that the spirit of true religion does not consist in selfish isolation from the world and in wrapt attention to inward wants and failings. It is to be found, on the contrary, wherever men are joined together in works of mutual aid and loving helpfulness, and it attains its sublimest and most truly Christian form only when *self* and selfish wants are thrown aside and forgotten, in devotion to the needs of others and submission to the Will of God.

Having now discussed at some length those objections to Confession and the doctrines commonly associated with it, which rest on their opposition to the spirit of social life, it is time for us to sum up shortly the general result at which we have arrived in the course of the preceding pages.

We found, it will be remembered, as the result of an enquiry into the laws and principles of moral progress, that there were *four* principal conditions which must be complied with before any institution can be pronounced good; and we have now seen that Confession fails to fulfil every one of these conditions.

It has been shewn, in the first place, that Confession is not likely to be resorted to only in cases where men are too weak or ignorant to act for themselves: but that its tendency, in the great majority of cases, will be to supersede self action and self reliance and to weaken the native force of the conscience and will.

Again, it has been pointed out, that, far from acting as a mere temporary discipline whose aim is to fit men gradually for the unassisted exercise of their own powers, Confession tends almost inevitably to perpetuate itself; and to tighten its hold on those who apply to it for assistance, so as to become at last an almost indispensable necessity of nature.

It has been shewn also that there is great danger of the true nature of Confession, as a human institution, being lost sight of, and that there is a constant temptation to regard it as a thing endowed with supernatural efficacy. Whenever this temptation is yielded to, a set of views and doctrines spring up which cannot fail to have a mischievous and degrading influence on men's characters. Motives and actions, dispositions and qualities, are tried by an altogether different standard from any that a moralist would set before him, and many of them, which are of the utmost value as *aids* to moral progress, are neglected and even purposely destroyed, because they cannot be made to fit in with the particular scheme of salvation which the Confessor has in view.

Thus far we had been concerned only with the *ethical* aspect of Confession, or with its *direct* effect on moral character. Passing thence to the *social* aspect of the question, we next proceeded to notice the effect which Confession would be likely to have upon the relations of family life: first pointing out the particular value of these relations in an ethical point of view, and then calling attention to the incompatibility between their spirit and that of the Confessional. The opposition between them we saw to be of the gravest and most important kind, and subsequent enquiry showed that there was a no less marked opposition between the Confessional and *political* institutions.

Lastly a brief sketch of the nature and moral characteristics of social life in general has brought us to the conclusion that the revival of Confession would be accompanied by a decline in all that is noblest and best in the intercourse of common life.

We have seen, therefore, that, judged as a human institution, Confession is likely to be both *morally* and *socially* injurious. It is to be condemned on the one hand for its direct effect upon character, and on the other hand for its *indirect* effects through its influence upon other institutions.

Its whole spirit and tendency, in short, are opposed to the true principles of moral progress, and, this being so, it can be of no avail to point to particular cases where it may not improbably work for good.

In the great majority of such cases the good

that would be done might be done nearly if not quite as well under the existing system, and in many English Parishes there can be no doubt that it *is* done.

Advice and sympathy can be given elsewhere than in the Confessional-box, and they will lose none of their value from coming spontaneously and as the need for them may be felt, instead of being dealt out at stated intervals in the forms and phrases which authority has prescribed.

As a matter of fact the formalities which Confessors delight in are hardly less destructive of true sympathy (without which there can be no real helpfulness) than is their isolation from worldly interests and common social intercourse on which all manuals on Confession insist so strongly[1].

This latter point furnishes material for one of the gravest charges that can be brought against the Confessional.

The easy relations which subsist at present

[1] "Seek detachment from all things, friends, property, pleasures, else the love of the world will soon draw you from the Road to Heaven." [Gaume's *Manual for Confessors*, Pusey's translation.]

between a clergyman and his parishioners are the source of much of the former's power for good, and they will be entirely done away with if the clergyman should be metamorphosed into the parish "*priest*" and Confessor.

It is not easy to measure the harm with which this change is likely to be attended, but it is certain that if clergymen are required to hold themselves aloof from the common life of their flock, the better part of their moral influence will be taken from them. The parochial clergy enjoy under the present system a power and opportunity of doing good such as it is given to few men to possess; and anything which should destroy this power or impair it in any serious degree, would in a *moral* point of view be nothing short of a national disaster. From the point of view of the "Sacramentalists" the matter will no doubt wear a different aspect.

The mysterious benefits of priestly absolution may perhaps be supposed to issue only from the seclusion and gloom of the Confessional: and, so far as this is what is wanted, it is natural that discontent should be felt with the existing state of things.

The working of the sacred machinery may very possibly require conditions which a clergyman mixing in the daily life of his parishioners would be unable to satisfy. The air of mystery and awe which should surround the privileged "Ambassador of Heaven" might suffer perhaps from a too frequent contact with those about him, and require to be kept up by various extrinsic aids. In short once admit the truth of the Sacramental theory of Confession, and all the objections we have been urging fall to the ground at once. The whole aspect of the question is changed and there is no longer anything unreasonable in the airs and pretensions which the Confessionalists love to affect. The moral influence of an ordinary clergyman over his flock will naturally, on this view, be held insignificant when compared with those diviner gifts which the Confessor has at his disposal, and common sense itself will dictate that the lesser benefit should be sacrificed to the greater.

All this, however, relates to matters on which a moralist as such feels himself to be quite incompetent to offer an opinion. It belongs to a region of thought which lies altogether beyond his reach, and, if he can succeed in depriving the "Sacramentalists" of the support of ethical arguments, he will have done all that can be required of him, and will be quite content to leave their general position unassailed. He has indeed no weapons with which to attack it, and may well be excused for shrinking from so unequal a contest.

This aspect of the question, then, we may safely leave in the hands of the theologians, resting satisfied with having pointed out the *moral* and *social* evils with which the revival of the Confession in England cannot fail to be attended.

APPENDIX.

SACRAMENTAL THEORY OF CONFESSION.

SACRAMENTAL Confession has been defined in the following way: "*Sacramentalis confessio* est quae fit illi qui habet aut habere creditur potestatem *absolvendi* cum animo se *peccatorem* accusandi et peccata sua *clavibus ecclesiae* subjiciendi, etiam si non sequatur absolutio." Billuart, Vol. IX. p. 445, *Dissert.* VIII. Art. 1.

Its nature again is clearly laid down in the Canons of Trent and in the Catechism of the Council founded on these Canons, as the following translation will shew. "Whosoever shall affirm that the Priest's Sacramental Absolution is not a *judicial* act, but only a ministry to declare and pronounce that the sins of the party confessing are forgiven, so that he believes himself absolved, even though the Priest should not absolve seriously, but in jesting; or shall affirm that the confession of the penitent is not necessary in order to obtain absolution from the Priest, let him be accursed. Whosoever shall affirm that Priests living in mortal sin have not the power of binding or loosing, or that Priests are not the *only ministers* of absolution, &c., let him be accursed." *Conc. Trid. Can.* 9, 10.

"In the minister of God who sits at the tribunal of penance, as his legitimate judge, he (the penitent) venerates the form and person of our Lord Jesus Christ; for in the administration of this, as in that of the other *sacraments*, the Priest *represents the character and dis-*

charges the functions of Jesus Christ." *Cat. Conc. Trid.* p. 260.

As Mr Boyd remarks (*Confession, Absolution, and the Real Presence*), "We can scarcely mistake the extent of this claim. If words have any meaning, these words must mean this, that the man declared pardoned is pardoned; that what has been loosed by the Priest on earth, has been loosed by Christ in heaven; that the recipient of priestly absolution goes away from the Confessional as fully forgiven as he would have been had our Lord, *and not man*, received his confession."

If it is objected that these are definitions taken from Roman Catholic sources, let us have the opinion of Anglican advocates of Confession.

"The Confessor," says the Rev. W. Gresley, "is to act in God's stead, whose Ambassador he is. He is like a judge pronouncing judgment, acquitting or else condemning, binding or loosing." *Ordinance of Confession*, p. 96.

Again, we are told by *The Priest in Absolution*, that "whatever theories people may form for themselves, the commission of absolution involves this restorative power (the pardon of sin after baptism) and is given to Priests of the English Church, the commission being of universal character and not confined to baptism, nay, if compared with the formula of the Roman Church, the English Ritual would seem the more prominently to set before the Priest as *his great work* that of binding and loosing."

Again, we quote from *Why don't you go to Confession?* "I must again repeat that Confession and Absolution form God's regular channel for conveying this forgiveness, and that if we will not take pardon in His way we are not likely to get it in our own." p. 9.

Again, we are told, "Just as God has appointed Baptism for forgiveness so has He most mercifully appointed a way—one way, and only one—for the certain forgiveness of sins committed after Baptism. That way, and I repeat that there is no other, is Sacramental Confession—Confession to a Priest." *Plain Words on Confession.*

Another writer goes so far as to speak of Confession as "the one covenanted means of forgiveness," and to quote with approval the statement that "The man who confesses to God *may* be forgiven; he who confesses to a Priest *must* be forgiven." *Six Plain Sermons*, by Rev. Wilkins, Priest.

Again, we have a clear avowal of belief in the Power of the Keys in *Books for the Young*, No. 1, Confession, "It is to the Priest, and to the Priest only, that a child must acknowledge his sins, if he desires that God should forgive him. Do you know why? It is because God, when He was on earth, gave to His Priests, and to them alone, the divine power of forgiving men their sins. Those who will not confess will not be cured."

Lastly, we may quote from evidence given in the *Rev. Alfred Poole's case.* "He said that I need not be afraid of telling him anything, for it would be kept strictly secret, and that God had given him power to remit or retain my sins." [Evidence of Eliz. Shiers.]

www.ingramcontent.com/pod-product-compliance
Lightning Source LLC
Chambersburg PA
CBHW020122170426
43199CB00009B/602